GOD MADE ME SPECIAL

written by Kristine K. Stewart
illustrated by Lorraine Arthur

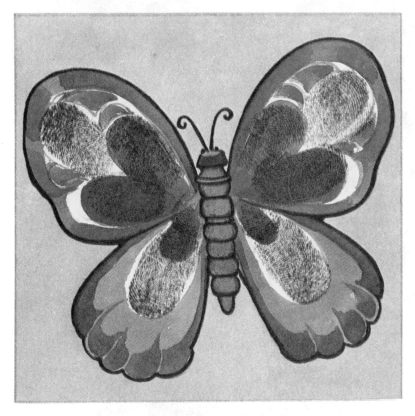

Thirteenth Printing, 1992
Library of Congress Catalog Card No. 82-62731
© 1983, The STANDARD PUBLISHING Company, Cincinnati, Ohio
Division of STANDEX INTERNATIONAL Corporation. Printed in U.S.A.

Hi! My name is Sarah. Mother and Daddy say that my thumbprint makes me extra special.

My thumbprint can become a bee
buzzing among the flowers.

But that's not why I'm special.

My thumbprint can become a bunch of
baby bunnies safe in their home
underground.

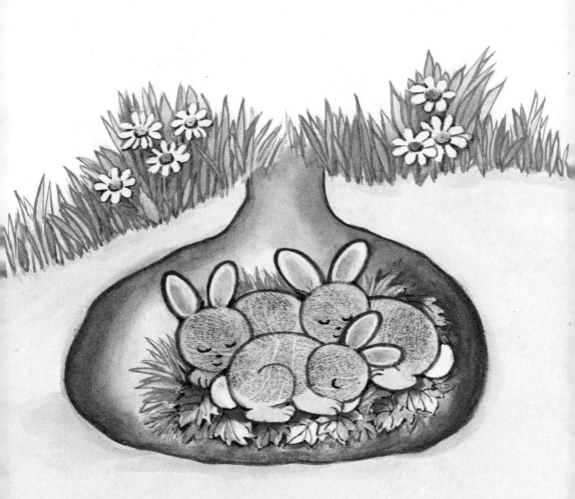

But that's not why I'm special.

My thumbprint can become a beautiful butterfly fluttering away from its cocoon.

But that's not why I'm special.

My thumbprint can become
a camel standing
comfortably in the
hot desert sun.

But that's not why I'm special.

My thumbprint can become a caterpillar
crawling through the grass.

But that's not why I'm special.

My thumbprint can become five chicks peeping in the sunshine.

But that's not why I'm special.

My thumbprint can become a duck
enjoying a spring shower.

But that's not why I'm special.

My thumbprint can become a herd of
elephants playing in the river.

But that's not why I'm special.

My thumbprint can become a frog, a turtle, and two polliwogs in a pond.

But that's not why I'm special.

My thumbprint can become a tall giraffe munching leaves from the top of a tree.

But that's not why I'm special.

My thumbprint can become a baby
kangaroo growing big and strong
inside its mother's pouch.

But that's not why I'm special.

My thumbprint can become a kitten
playing with a ball of string.

But that's not why I'm special.

My thumbprint
can become
a koala
munching
on juicy
eucalyptus
leaves.

But that's not why I'm special.

My thumbprint can become a lazy lion lounging in the sunlight.

But that's not why I'm special.

My thumbprint can become three little mice nibbling on some cheese.

But that's not why I'm special.

My thumbprint can become
two owls perched on a
limb.

But that's not why I'm special.

My thumbprint can become a family of
pigs with squiggly tails.

But that's not why I'm special.

My thumbprint can become a grumpy,
old spider spinning its web.

But that's not why I'm special.

My thumbprint can become a teddy bear on my pillow.

But that's not why I'm special.

I'm special because God made my thumbprint so that no one else in the whole world would have one

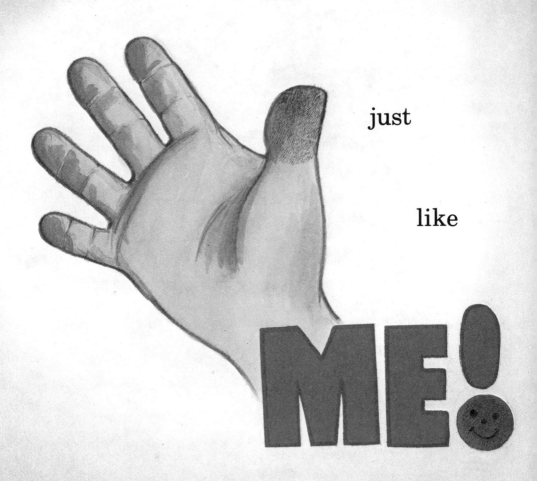

just

like

What can your thumbprint become?